THE CONTENTMENT NOTEBOOK

SIMPLE REFLECTIONS FOR BUSY LIVES

The Contentment Notebook is designed as a daily companion for individuals navigating the intricacies of everyday life. Through a series of thoughtfully crafted prompts and illustrations, it offers users an opportunity to reflect on various aspects of their lives, from personal relationships and career choices to hobbies and spiritual beliefs. By facilitating consistent introspection, the notebook aims to help people identify areas of contentment and areas that may need adjustment. In doing so, it promotes a holistic approach to well-being, encouraging users to maintain a balanced life filled with both purpose and pleasure.

THE CONTENTMENT NOTEBOOK

"Welcome to the start of something for you. Every person's life is distinct, punctuated with moments of joy, challenges, discoveries, and revelations. Yet, amid the rush of busy lives and daily tasks, many of us often lose sight of the little pockets of contentment that silently weave the fabric of our days. That's where The Contentment Notebook steps in."

What's the big deal about contentment ?

Being content isn't about having a constant smile plastered on your face. It's more about recognizing and appreciating the good bits of your day, even if it's just for a moment. A sense of contentment, often regarded as a deep-seated state of satisfaction and well-being, is associated with a variety of psychological, emotional, and physical benefits. Here are some areas where having a greater sense of contentment may be beneficial for you.

- Improved Relationships:

Content individuals tend to have healthier relationships because they are less likely to project their frustrations onto others. Their calm and positive demeanor can also foster deeper connections with others.

- Greater Resilience:

Contentment cultivates a perspective that enables people to cope better with adversities. When they face challenges, content individuals are often more resilient and are able to bounce back quicker.

- Clearer Decision Making:

When you're content, you're less likely to make decisions based on emotional impulses or external pressures. Instead, you're more apt to make thoughtful and constructive choices.

- Higher Productivity:

Contentment can lead to better focus and efficiency. Without the constant search for more or better, you can direct your energy into meaningful tasks and projects.

- Increased Creativity:

Being at peace with oneself and one's circumstances can create a mental space conducive to creativity. Without the clutter of dissatisfaction, the mind is free to wander and come up with innovative ideas.

- Personal Growth:

Contentment doesn't mean complacency. In fact, it can fuel personal growth. When you're content, you're more likely to pursue activities and goals that contribute to your development.

- Improved Sleep:

Discontent can lead to rumination and anxiety, which disrupt sleep. A peaceful and contented mind often translates to better sleep quality.

- Enhanced Enjoyment of Life:

Contentment allows individuals to savor the present moment, making them more appreciative of the small joys and experiences life offers.

- Less Materialism:

A content individual is less likely to seek happiness in material possessions. This can lead to a more sustainable and environmentally friendly lifestyle.

- Better Financial Health:

With reduced desires to 'keep up with the Joneses,' contented individuals often make more sustainable financial decisions, avoiding unnecessary debt and impulse purchases.

In summary, contentment can enhance nearly every aspect of one's life, from physical and mental well-being to relationships and financial stability. It's a holistic state of well-being that can lead to a more fulfilled, balanced, and meaningful life.

How this notebook could help ?

This notebook is your space, to use as you like. This isn't a "do this, do that" kind of book. Think of it as a space to jot down thoughts on various bits of your life. Job, family, hobbies, even how you spend you money – it's all here.

You'll find prompts touching different areas of your life. Three gentle nudges per page. Dive into them as you like. Some days you might tackle all three; other days, just one will do. Or none! That's fine too.

Every page space to mark the date. It's there if you want to remember when you scribbled down your thoughts. Occasionally, as you work through the days, there's a spot prompting you for any 'aha!' moments or reflections. A sort of 'how you doing?' moment to review your progress.

What areas are we thinking about?

Each of the aspects listed below provides a mirror to reflect upon our lives, ensuring that we're not only living but thriving in every possible way.

- Career:

Our careers are more than just jobs; they're reflections of our passions and values. Evaluating job satisfaction, looking at growth opportunities, and checking the alignment with personal passions can help us find deeper meaning and purpose in what we do. Feeling content in our career often translates to happiness in other areas of life.

- Finances:

Financial well-being is more than numbers; it's about the peace of mind that comes from feeling secure. Reflecting on budgets, savings, and overall financial health allows us to make empowered decisions, leading to a sense of control and contentment.

- Health and Fitness:

Taking a moment to appreciate our bodies and evaluate our physical and mental well-being reminds us of the importance of self-care. From the food we eat to the exercise routines we maintain, nurturing our body and mind brings intrinsic rewards of vitality and contentment.

- Relationships:

The bonds we share with family, friends, and partners add depth to our lives. By exploring these connections, we can nurture healthier dynamics, appreciate the support systems we have, and make conscious efforts to strengthen our ties.

- Personal Growth:

Life is an endless journey of learning and evolving. Reflecting on our growth areas, from skills to personal traits, helps us recognize our progress. It's a reminder that every effort, big or small, contributes to our ever-evolving self.

- Family Dynamics:

Families are complex, but they're our anchor. Assessing our relationships within the family, understanding communication patterns, and addressing issues paves the way for a more harmonious and supportive home environment.

- Social Life:

Human beings are social creatures. By examining our social activities and connections, we can ensure that we're fostering meaningful relationships that uplift, inspire, and bring joy.

- Hobbies and Interests:

The activities that resonate with our hearts bring unmatched joy. Whether it's a hobby, a passion project, or a simple pastime, these interests add colour to our lives, helping us recharge and express ourselves.

- Spirituality/Inner Life:

Our inner world guides our external actions. Reflecting on our spiritual beliefs, practicing mindfulness, or seeking inner peace allows us to navigate life with grace and purpose, ensuring a deeper sense of fulfilment.

- Our Environment:

Our surroundings significantly influence our mood. From the home's decor to its tidiness, evaluating our living spaces can help us create an environment that's conducive to productivity, relaxation, and happiness.

- Community Involvement:

Giving back is a profound source of contentment. By engaging in community activities and volunteering, we strengthen our bond with society and derive a sense of purpose that extends beyond our individual lives.

- Work-Life Balance:

Balance is key. Reflecting on how we juggle work responsibilities with leisure and relaxation ensures that we're living a life that's both productive and enriching.

- Time Management:

Time is our most precious resource. Assessing our time management skills helps us maximize our days, ensuring we're giving due attention to all facets of our life.

- Communication Skills:

Effective communication fosters understanding. By evaluating our expression and listening skills, we can build stronger, more transparent relationships in every sphere of life.

- Goal Achievement:

Goals guide our journey. Reflecting on our achievements, both big and small, fills us with pride and motivates us to keep pushing forward.

- Creativity and Expression:

Every individual has a unique voice. Through creative outlets, we find a platform to express ourselves, adding layers of depth to our identity and bringing immense satisfaction.

- Learning and Curiosity:

Embracing new knowledge keeps us vibrant. Celebrating our curiosity and love for learning ensures we're always evolving, both intellectually and personally.

- Emotional Well-being:

Emotional health is paramount. By understanding our emotional triggers, learning coping mechanisms, and practicing self-compassion, we cultivate a resilient spirit that's equipped to handle life's highs and lows.

- Adventure and Exploration:

The world is vast and waiting to be explored. Whether it's a new hobby, a trip, or a simple change in routine, embracing new experiences adds excitement and depth to our life narrative.

- Contribution to Society:

Our legacy is defined by the impact we leave behind. Reflecting on our contributions, both big and small, reminds us of our potential to make a difference, instilling a sense of purpose and pride.

Some Friendly Tips

- Don't rush. This isn't a race. Some days you'll have lots to say; other times, a word or two will do.
- There's no "perfect answer". This is just about your thoughts and feelings.
- There may be some prompts that just don't work for you, that's ok... just leave them and move on!
- Enjoy the process. Over time, you'll see patterns, learn more about yourself, and maybe even raise a smile at things you hadn't noticed before.

Alright, Let's Dive In!

Remember, this notebook is your space, and there's no wrong way to use it. It's a tool, a friend, a confidante. So settle in, take a deep breath, and let's explore the contentment in your life, one page at a time.

THE CONTENTMENT NOTEBOOK

SIMPLE REFLECTIONS FOR BUSY LIVES

Date

- How have family dynamics shifted over time?
- Do I have a budget, and if so, how closely do I stick to it?
- Am I open to adapting or evolving my hobbies over time?

Date

- Are there opportunities for me to share my own culture or experiences with the community?
- Are there times when work seems to overshadow other areas of my life?
- Have I mentored or helped someone in their personal or career growth?

Date ____________

- Do I set aside time for self-reflection and personal planning?
- Is my work-life balance conducive to my physical and mental well-being?
- How can I create a daily routine that better serves my needs?

Date ____________

- Do I have mentors or people I learn from regularly?
- How can I make my living space more eco-friendly?
- Do I have enough time for self-care and relaxation?

Date ____________

- How does my time management affect my stress levels?
- Do I have any debts, and what's my plan for managing them?
- How do I incorporate a sense of exploration in my daily life?

Date ____________

- What platforms do I have to voice social concerns?
- What skills have I gained through my goal-achieving efforts?
- Is it easy for me to "switch off" from work mode when I'm at home?

Date ____________

- Do I have a bucket list? What's on it?
- Do I feel connected to nature in my living environment?
- How does my living environment impact my daily routines?

Date ____________

- Do I feel supported by my employer in maintaining a work-life balance?
- How can I make my community more inclusive or welcoming?
- What's a past contribution I'm particularly proud of?

Date ____________

- Are there toxic relationships I need to address or let go of?
- Am I continually seeking to expand my horizons and learn new things?
- What is my relationship with substances like alcohol, tobacco, or caffeine?

Date ___________

- Are there any subscriptions or recurring expenses I can trim down?
- What have I learned from my mistakes?
- Are there toxic relationships I need to address or let go of?

Date ____________

- Have I received constructive feedback lately, and how have I acted on it?
- Are my goals aligned with my values and passions?
- What activities help me unwind after a busy day at work?

Date ____________

- Am I setting SMART goals (Specific, Measurable, Achievable, Relevant, Time-bound)?
- Is it easy for me to "switch off" from work mode when I'm at home?
- How do I maintain a balance between my inner and outer worlds?

Date ____________

- Are there any self-limiting beliefs holding me back?
- What future initiatives do I want to be a part of?
- What steps can I take to achieve better work-life harmony?

Date ____________

- Am I able to say no to extra tasks or projects that would disrupt my work-life balance?
- Do I support local businesses and initiatives?
- Am I making the most of tax-advantaged savings accounts?

Date ____________

- How does my current lifestyle fit within my income?
- How am I investing in my own well-being and happiness?
- How can I involve my friends or family in charitable activities?

Date ____________

- Do I feel supported and uplifted by my friends?
- What are the milestones or achievements I'm most proud of this year?
- Do I actively listen when someone else is speaking?

Date ____________

- How comfortable do I feel in social settings?
- Looking forward, what changes would I like to make to improve my financial well-being?
- How do I manage stress and what coping mechanisms work best for me?

Date ____________

- Am I compassionate towards myself when I make a mistake?
- Are there mentors or role models at work who inspire me?
- Could I dedicate a specific amount of time each month to community involvement?

Date ____________

- Do I feel valued and respected in my workplace?
- Do I carry any family-related stress or anxiety?
- Looking forward, what changes would I like to make to improve my financial well-being?

Date ___________

- What are some non-material things that make me happy?
- Do I feel in control of my financial destiny?
- Am I good at estimating how long tasks will take?

Date ___________

- How does my creativity influence my perspective on the world?
- How does giving back to the community make me feel?
- How do I contribute to the well-being and happiness of others in my life?

Date ___________

- How do I engage with my emotions, rather than suppressing them?
- Are there any 'time sinks' in my personal life that could be better spent?
- Could I be a bridge in bringing different communities together?

Date ____________

- Are my investments diversified to help me meet my future needs?
- How do my relationships affect my mental and emotional state?
- What are some small joys that lift my spirits?

Date ____________

- What are the common distractions that derail my focus and how can I manage them?
- How do my hobbies impact my financial well-being?
- How do I handle social pressures or expectations?

Date ___________

- How often do I check my work emails or attend to work tasks outside of official work hours?
- How do I contribute to the well-being of my friends?
- How can I amplify the voices of those less heard in society?

Date ______________

- Do I give constructive feedback to others?
- Do I make time for hobbies and activities that bring me joy?
- Do I feel a sense of community and belonging in my social circles?

Date ______________

- Can I give more of my time, resources, or skills?
- Do I share what I learn with others?
- What organizations or causes would I like to support?

REVIEW MOMENT

HOW CONSISTENT HAVE I BEEN IN USING THE CONTENTMENT NOTEBOOK?

Consistency is key when it comes to reflection and personal growth. Take a moment to think about how often you've been engaging with the notebook. Are you meeting your own expectations, or is there room for improvement?

Date ____________

- How can I involve my friends or family in charitable activities?
- Am I making the most of tax-advantaged savings accounts?
- What steps can I take if I feel like work is starting to encroach on my personal life?

Date ____________

- Are there financial discussions or decisions I've been avoiding?
- How do I handle not knowing something?
- Do I have a go-to method for de-stressing after a long day?

Date ____________

- How often do I find myself scrambling to meet deadlines?
- How have family dynamics shifted over time?
- How do I show appreciation and love to those who matter most to me?

Date ___________

- Do I have any unresolved conflicts at work, and what can I do about them?
- How satisfied am I with my current social circle?
- What was the last book I read, and what did I learn from it?

Date ___________

- How do I stay grounded when faced with stress or external pressures?
- How much time do I allocate for unplanned interruptions or delays?
- How do I generally feel when I wake up in the morning?

Date ____________

- How do I incorporate creativity into my daily life?
- What expectations do I have for my relationships, and are they realistic?
- How knowledgeable am I about financial topics, and where could I improve?

Date ____________

- How often do I check in with myself emotionally?
- What piece of art, music, or literature has inspired me recently?
- How has my involvement in the community enriched my life?

Date ____________

- How often do I participate in community events or projects?
- What piece of art, music, or literature has inspired me recently?
- What role does intimacy play in my life, and am I content with it?

Date ____________

- Am I clear and concise when conveying my thoughts?
- Do I feel valued and respected in my workplace?
- How comfortable do I feel in social settings?

Date ____________

- Do I take time to understand others' viewpoints before responding?
- Do I have a "travel tribe" or people who encourage me to explore?
- Do I feel connected to my neighbourhood or local community?

Date ___________

- Do I actively listen when someone else is speaking?
- Do I know my neighbours and community members on a first-name basis?
- Do I ever use my creativity to solve problems at work or home?

Date ___________

- What qualities do I admire in my family, and which could be improved?
- How do I maintain boundaries in my relationships?
- What creative outlets bring me the most joy?

Date ____________

- How do I incorporate a sense of exploration in my daily life?
- How does my family handle crises or challenges?
- What changes do I wish to see in society?

Date ______________

- Are there mentors, texts, or philosophies that inspire my spiritual journey?
- What online or community resources do I use for learning?
- Am I fairly compensated for the work I do?

Date ______________

- What quality time have I spent with loved ones recently?
- How informed am I about current events and social issues?
- Do I prioritize my to-dos, or do I tend to react to what comes up?

Date ______

- What personal goals have I set for myself, and what's my plan to achieve them?
- Do I feel supported and uplifted by my friends?
- What resources could help me achieve my goals faster?

Date ______

- What goals have I set for myself this year?
- Do I balance time between family, work, and social life?
- What are some ways I can be more eco-friendly?

Date ___________

- Am I taking steps to manage stress and build resilience?
- Do I have a designated space for relaxation and self-care?
- How do my hobbies impact my financial well-being?

Date ___________

- What barriers have I overcome in reaching my goals?
- How do I handle moral or ethical dilemmas?
- Am I comfortable setting boundaries in different areas of my life?

Date ___________

- How often do I engage in mindfulness practices like meditation or deep-breathing exercises?
- Do I often initiate plans or wait to be invited?
- Are there changes I could make in my daily routine that would improve my balance?

Date ____________

- How do I currently feel about my work-life balance?
- What can I do to make my home more peaceful?
- What quality time have I spent with loved ones recently?

Date ____________

- Do I feel guilty taking time off work? If so, why?
- How do I generally feel when I wake up in the morning?
- Are my goals aligned with my values and passions?

Date ___________

- Am I able to be my authentic self in my relationships?
- Are there differences in values or beliefs that cause tension?
- What role does exercise play in my life, and is it a positive one?

Date ____________

- Am I generally persuasive when I want to be?
- What steps can I take to better align my actions with my inner values?
- Are there any small changes I can make to improve my living environment?

Date ____________

- Do I ever use my creativity to solve problems at work or home?
- Do I have opportunities for promotion or lateral moves in my current role?
- Have I considered turning a hobby into a side hustle?

Date ___________

- How can I make my community more inclusive or welcoming?
- Do I tailor my communication style to suit different audiences?
- Am I satisfied with how much time I spend on leisure activities?

Date ___________

- How often do I reassess my daily or weekly schedule?
- Do I regularly celebrate my own progress, however small it may be?
- Do I balance time between family, work, and social life?

Date ___________

- How do I handle setbacks or failures?
- How do I generally feel about my current time management skills?
- How do I handle conflict within my relationships?

REVIEW MOMENT

WHAT SURPRISING INSIGHTS HAVE I GAINED SO FAR?

Sometimes the act of reflection can lead to unexpected realizations about ourselves. Have any of the prompts led you to discover something new or surprising? These insights can be enlightening waypoints on your journey to contentment.

Date ____________

- What's a local spot I haven't explored but would like to?
- How do I reinforce or apply new knowledge?
- What physical activities bring me joy and fulfilment?

Date ____________

- How do the ethics and values of my workplace align with my own?
- What are some of the things I've always wanted to do but haven't yet?
- What financial milestones have I reached, and what's next on the horizon?

Date ______________

- How does the layout of my home affect its functionality?
- How do I handle setbacks or failures?
- What aspects of my job make me feel most fulfilled?

Date ______________

- Are there tasks that I could delegate or outsource to free up more time?
- In what small ways do I contribute to my community?
- Do I feel like I have enough "me-time"?

Date ____________

- How well do I manage my emotions while communicating?
- What platforms do I have to voice social concerns?
- Do I have a bucket list? What's on it?

Date ___________

- What is one emotional well-being goal I'd like to set for myself this month?
- What's a skill I've always wanted to learn?
- What changes do I wish to see in society?

Date ___________

- What's one activity that I wish I had more time for?
- What are the strongest virtues I try to cultivate?
- How do I feel after spending time on my hobbies?

Date ____________

- Do I feel supported and understood by the people around me?
- What's one action I can take this week to improve my communication skills?
- Could I benefit from setting more specific deadlines for my tasks?

Date ____________

- What's a local spot I haven't explored but would like to?
- Am I compassionate towards myself when I make a mistake?
- Are there specific areas, like work or home, where I think my communication could improve?

Date ___________

- Do I have any adventure or exploration goals for this year?
- Am I satisfied with how much time I spend on leisure activities?
- How can I better support my family members?

Date ___________

- What's one new place I'd like to visit this year?
- Are there toxic relationships I need to address or let go of?
- What acts of kindness have I engaged in recently?

Date ___________

- Do I feel emotionally connected to my community or social circle?
- What's a small adventure I can go on this weekend?
- How do I handle moral or ethical dilemmas?

Date ___________

- Do I make time for hobbies and activities that bring me joy?
- What does self-care look like for me?
- Am I able to be my authentic self in my relationships?

Date ___________

- Am I excited to go to work most days, or is it a struggle?
- How can I involve my friends or family in charitable activities?
- How well do I balance emotional giving and receiving in my relationships?

Date ________________

- How have my values and priorities changed over time?
- How do I show appreciation and love to those who matter most to me?
- What can I do to make my home more peaceful?

Date ___________

- How do I maintain a balance between my inner and outer worlds?
- How does my creativity influence my perspective on the world?
- Do I feel a sense of community and belonging in my social circles?

Date ___________

- Who or what motivates me to reach my goals?
- Am I able to be my authentic self in my relationships?
- How can I use my skills to benefit others?

Date ______________

- What creative achievements am I most proud of?
- What personal goals have I set for myself, and what's my plan to achieve them?
- How do I generally feel about my current time management skills?

Date ______________

- What's the one hobby I would pursue if time and money were not a constraint?
- Am I investing time in deepening existing relationships?
- What would I like my lasting impact on society to be?

Date ____________

- Have I mentored or helped someone in their personal or career growth?
- How often do I participate in community events or projects?
- How can I make my workspace more conducive to productivity, so work doesn't spill into personal time?

Date ______________

- Do I know my neighbours and community members on a first-name basis?
- Are there spiritual or mindfulness practices I want to learn more about?
- Do I have opportunities for promotion or lateral moves in my current role?

Date ______________

- Is my current work-life balance sustainable?
- Am I keeping up with regular health check-ups and screenings?
- How do I contribute to a positive family environment?

Date ____________

- What financial milestones have I reached, and what's next on the horizon?
- Is there a local issue that I feel strongly about and want to address?
- How often do I experience feelings of fatigue or burnout?

Date ____________

- How am I investing in my own well-being and happiness?
- How do I maintain a positive mindset when faced with challenges?
- What local organizations could benefit from my skills or time?

Date __________

- What's stopping me from taking the next step towards a big adventure?
- Am I generally persuasive when I want to be?
- Are there friendships that need rekindling?

Date ______

- How does my work-life balance affect my relationships?
- How often do I dedicate time to my hobbies?
- Are there any financial worries that keep me up at night?

Date ______

- What steps have I taken to improve my mental health?
- How do the ethics and values of my workplace align with my own?
- How secure do I feel about my current financial situation?

REVIEW MOMENT

ARE THERE AREAS IN THE NOTEBOOK WHERE I FIND MYSELF SPENDING MORE TIME? WHY DO I THINK THAT IS?

You may notice that some sections resonate more with you than others. Spend some time pondering why certain areas attract more of your attention. This could reveal aspects of your life that you subconsciously prioritize.

Date ________

- How does my body language align with my verbal communication?
- Do I have the flexibility in my work schedule to attend to personal matters?
- Do I feel emotionally connected to my community or social circle?

Date ________

- What traditions or rituals are important to our family identity?
- How can I use my skills to benefit others?
- How satisfied am I with my current social circle?

Date ______________

- Are there changes I could make in my daily routine that would improve my balance?
- Do I share my creative works with others? Why or why not?
- Do I feel in control of my financial destiny?

Date ____________

- What physical activities bring me joy and fulfilment?
- Do I feel supported by my employer in maintaining a work-life balance?
- Does my living space feel cluttered or disorganized?

Date ____________

- How has my perspective broadened through past adventures?
- How does my living environment impact my daily routines?
- What small acts of kindness could I easily integrate into my daily life?

Date ____________

- What was the last book I read, and what did I learn from it?
- How do I handle setbacks or challenges in my health journey?
- Do I tailor my communication style to suit different audiences?

Date ____________

- Do I have enough time for self-care and relaxation?
- Are there aspects of my job that make it difficult to maintain a healthy balance?
- What's one small creative act I can do today?

Date __________

- What emotions or thoughts frequently occupy my inner world?
- How well do I communicate under pressure?
- How often do I engage in social activities that bring me joy?

Date ________

- What's one step I could take right now toward a goal?
- Do the objects and decor in my home bring me joy?
- Are there unresolved issues with family or friends that weigh on my mind?

Date ________

- Are there aspects of my job that make it difficult to maintain a healthy balance?
- How do I feel mentally and emotionally on most days?
- How do I react to criticism or differing opinions?

Date ____________

- Am I afraid of judgment or criticism for my creative work?
- What are some small joys that lift my spirits?
- How do I educate myself on issues of social justice?

Date ____________

- Have I mentored or helped someone in their personal or career growth?
- What are some character traits I'm proud of?
- Do I feel like I'm in touch with my emotional self?

Date ____________

- Do I support local businesses and initiatives?
- What's a local spot I haven't explored but would like to?
- How do I handle social pressures or expectations?

Date ____________

- How often do I practice gratitude?
- Are there specific areas, like work or home, where I think my communication could improve?
- What cultural experiences have I always wanted to immerse myself in?

Date ____________

- How do I maintain a positive mindset when faced with challenges?
- What's one new place I'd like to visit this year?
- What steps can I take to nurture closer, healthier family relationships?

Date

- How do I reinforce or apply new knowledge?
- Do I reward myself when I achieve a goal?
- Do I feel supported by my employer in maintaining a work-life balance?

Date

- How do our family dynamics impact my well-being?
- What's one small creative act I can do today?
- What are some happy memories that bring the family together?

Date ____________

- What role does intimacy play in my life, and am I content with it?
- How do I balance ambition with contentment?
- What creative achievements am I most proud of?

Date ______________

- How often do I communicate digitally vs. face-to-face, and does the medium matter to me?
- What creative outlets bring me the most joy?
- How much of my identity is tied to my career, and is that okay with me?

Date ______________

- Am I open to adapting or evolving my hobbies over time?
- Are there financial discussions or decisions I've been avoiding?
- Do I have a support system that understands and respects my health goals?

Date ____________

- Do I set aside time for self-reflection and personal planning?
- What barriers have I overcome in reaching my goals?
- How often do I dedicate time to my hobbies?

Date ____________

- Do my hobbies challenge me in beneficial ways?
- Do I feel a sense of belonging in my social groups?
- What's a skill I've always wanted to learn?

Date ____________

- Looking forward, what changes would I like to make to improve my financial well-being?
- Could my hobbies lead to new social or career opportunities?
- Am I taking steps to manage stress and build resilience?

Date ____________

- Am I drinking enough water and staying properly hydrated?
- How does my work-life balance affect my relationships?
- What expectations do I have for my relationships, and are they realistic?

Date ____________

- Are there times when work seems to overshadow other areas of my life?
- Is there a diversity of perspectives and experiences within my social circle?
- How often do I participate in community events or projects?

Date ____________

- How do I feel about my current communication skills?
- What steps can I take if I feel like work is starting to encroach on my personal life?
- Do I share any hobbies with friends or family?

Date ____________

- Are there any small changes I can make to improve my living environment?
- How often do I check my work emails or attend to work tasks outside of official work hours?
- Do my hobbies allow me to express my creativity?

Date ___________

- How can I better support my family members?
- How effective am I at resolving conflicts through communication?
- How does my inner life influence my daily actions?

REVIEW MOMENT

HOW DO I FEEL ABOUT MY JOURNEY TOWARD CONTENTMENT AT THIS STAGE?

Periodic emotional check-ins are important. Are you feeling optimistic, overwhelmed, or perhaps indifferent about your journey? Your emotional temperature can offer clues about what you need to focus on next.

Date ____________

- Do I have a sleep routine that leaves me feeling rested and rejuvenated?
- Are there changes I could make in my daily routine that would improve my balance?
- What are some non-material things that make me happy?

Date ____________

- Are there causes or issues in my community that I'm passionate about?
- What aspects of communication do I find challenging?
- Am I fairly compensated for the work I do?

Date ____________

- What new social activities or groups would I like to explore?
- What are some small joys that lift my spirits?
- Have I achieved any milestones toward my long-term goals recently?

Date ____________

- How well do I communicate under pressure?
- Do I have a dedicated space for work, relaxation, and hobbies?
- How do I stay grounded when faced with stress or external pressures?

Date ___________

- What boundaries have I set, and are they respected?
- Are there specific rooms or spaces where I feel most content?
- Do my hobbies challenge me in beneficial ways?

Date ______

- Do my social activities align with my values and interests?
- Is there a difference between my public persona and my inner self?
- How do I handle not knowing something?

Date ______

- How do I handle not knowing something?
- What activities or routines make me feel centred?
- Is there a diversity of perspectives and experiences within my social circle?

Date __________

- What are some ways I can volunteer that align with my interests?
- Have I received constructive feedback lately, and how have I acted on it?
- Do I often initiate plans or wait to be invited?

Date __________

- What expectations do I have for my relationships, and are they realistic?
- Are there any financial worries that keep me up at night?
- How do weekends and days off look for me? Restorative or just an extension of work?

Date ____________

- Do I tailor my communication style to suit different audiences?
- Am I able to say no to extra tasks or projects that would disrupt my work-life balance?
- What is one financial habit I'm proud of?

Date ____________

- Do I have plants or natural elements that contribute to a sense of well-being?
- Am I drinking enough water and staying properly hydrated?
- How do I incorporate creativity into my daily life?

Date ____________

- How informed am I about current events and social issues?
- What steps can I take to improve the quality of my social life?
- Is my current work-life balance sustainable?

Date ____________

- What activities or routines make me feel centred?
- Do I ask for feedback on how I can communicate better?
- How can I involve my family or friends in community activities?

Date ____________

- How do I handle conflict within my relationships?
- How do I engage with my emotions, rather than suppressing them?
- Do I have a "travel tribe" or people who encourage me to explore

Date ____________

- Do I have a dedicated space for work, relaxation, and hobbies?
- How well do I balance emotional giving and receiving in my relationships?
- How much time do I allocate for unplanned interruptions or delays?

Date ____________

- Are there specific rooms or spaces where I feel most content?
- Do I feel more energized or relaxed after expressing myself creatively?
- Do I feel a sense of belonging in my social groups?

Date ____________

- How can I create a daily routine that better serves my needs?
- Do I engage in practices that promote mental clarity?
- How do I react when things don't go as planned?

Date ______________

- Am I satisfied with the quality of time spent with family?
- How satisfied am I with my current level of physical fitness?
- How often do I engage in deep, meaningful conversations?

Date ______________

- How do I feel when I check my bank account or financial statements?
- How do I manage stress and what coping mechanisms work best for me?
- Do I give constructive feedback to others?

Date ___________

- How often do I find myself in misunderstandings?
- What activities help me unwind after a busy day at work?
- Are there specific rooms or spaces where I feel most content?

Date ______________

- Do I balance time between family, work, and social life?
- How does the layout of my home affect its functionality?
- Are there any changes I'd like to make to my outdoor living space?

Date ______________

- What online or community resources do I use for learning?
- How do my spending habits align with my values?
- Do I have a dedicated space for work, relaxation, and hobbies?

Date __________

- How do I maintain boundaries in my relationships?
- Do I set clear boundaries between work time and personal time?
- What's a topic I'd like to know more about but have hesitated to dive into?

Date __________

- Am I willing to unlearn beliefs or habits that are no longer useful?
- How often do I check in with myself emotionally?
- How do new experiences make me feel?

Date ____________

- Could my hobbies lead to new social or career opportunities?
- Are there any persistent health issues or symptoms that I should address?
- Do I have a designated space for relaxation and self-care?

Date ____________

- How can I make my living space more eco-friendly?
- How do I incorporate a sense of exploration in my daily life?
- Are there tasks that consistently take longer than I expect?

Date ____________

- How does my time management impact people around me?
- Do I have a specific action plan for each of my goals?
- Are there aspects of my job that make it difficult to maintain a healthy balance?

REVIEW MOMENT

HAVE I SHARED ANY OF MY REFLECTIONS OR DISCOVERIES WITH SOMEONE CLOSE TO ME?

Sharing your journey can make it more fulfilling and can also provide you with valuable external perspectives. Consider if you've involved friends or family and what their reactions have been.

Date ____________

- Do my hobbies allow me to escape and recharge effectively?
- Do I share what I learn with others?
- Do I feel a sense of duty or obligation, and is it balanced?

Date ____________

- Are there any new interests I'd like to explore?
- Do I make time for self-directed learning outside of work or school?
- Are there unresolved issues that need addressing?

Date ____________

- Am I open to exploring different artistic mediums?
- Are there aspects of my life where I feel stuck, and what can I do about it?
- How can I amplify the voices of those less heard in society?

Date ____________

- What are some of the things I've always wanted to do but haven't yet?
- What barriers keep me from being more creative?
- When was the last time I did something for the first time?

Date ____________

- Have I considered ethical aspects of my spending habits?
- What steps can I take to achieve better work-life harmony?
- Am I often late, and if so, why?

Date ____________

- How do I handle setbacks or challenges in my health journey?
- What's one small step I can take this week to satisfy my curiosity in a particular area?
- Do I have a specific action plan for each of my goals?

Date ____________

- Do I have mentors, role models, or guides who enrich my perspective?
- How often do I step out of my comfort zone?
- What small victories should I celebrate today?

Date ______________

- When was the last time I did something for the first time?
- Am I mindful of my emotional energy and where it goes?
- What are the strongest virtues I try to cultivate?

Date ___________

- Do I carry any family-related stress or anxiety?
- How do I incorporate creativity into my daily life?
- Could my hobbies lead to new social or career opportunities?

Date ___________

- How does my family handle crises or challenges?
- How would I describe my personal belief system?
- Am I compassionate towards myself when I make a mistake?

Date __________

- Do I have a designated space for relaxation and self-care?
- Am I setting SMART goals (Specific, Measurable, Achievable, Relevant, Time-bound)?
- What's a creative project I've been putting off?

Date __________

- Am I clear about why each goal is important to me?
- Are there people in my life who encourage my creativity?
- Do I have a budget, and if so, how closely do I stick to it?

Date ____________

- How do my hobbies impact my financial well-being?
- What's a creative project I've been putting off?
- Am I investing time in deepening existing relationships?

Date ______________

- How do I contribute to the well-being and happiness of others in my life?
- Do I have any long-term learning goals?
- Is there a local issue that I feel strongly about and want to address?

Date ______________

- How do I maintain a positive mindset when faced with challenges?
- What practices help me find inner peace?
- What are some ways I can volunteer that align with my interests?

Date __________

- How has my involvement in the community enriched my life?
- Are there mentors, texts, or philosophies that inspire my spiritual journey?
- Am I open to feedback, and do I use it as an opportunity for growth?

Date __________

- Do I have the flexibility in my work schedule to attend to personal matters?
- Have I discovered any new forms of creativity recently?
- What's a small adventure I can go on this weekend?

Date ____________

- Do my work responsibilities play to my strengths?
- How often do I engage in social activities that bring me joy?
- How do my goals affect my daily routines and habits?

Date ____________

- How do I measure my own success, and is that metric fulfilling?
- Do I have mentors, role models, or guides who enrich my perspective?
- What skills would I like to develop to advance in my career?

Date ____________

- How do I keep up-to-date with news and trends in areas I care about?
- Have I achieved any milestones toward my long-term goals recently?
- What activities or routines make me feel centred?

Date ____________

- Is there a balance between solitary and social hobbies?
- How can I create a daily routine that better serves my needs?
- What's one step I could take right now toward a goal?

Date ____________

- Do I reward myself when I achieve a goal?
- What was the last book I read, and what did I learn from it?
- How can I make my community more inclusive or welcoming?

Date ____________

- Are there barriers that prevent me from being more active in community initiatives?
- Do I use any tools or techniques to manage my time better?
- Do I have any debts, and what's my plan for managing them?

Date ____________

- How effective am I at resolving conflicts through communication?
- Do I have a bucket list? What's on it?
- What new skills have I learned recently?

Date ____________

- How often do I find myself in misunderstandings?
- Am I excited to go to work most days, or is it a struggle?
- What have I learned from my hobbies?

Date ___________

- Are there toxic or draining relationships that I should reconsider?
- How can I better support my family members?
- Have I discovered any new forms of creativity recently?

Date ___________

- Are there any new interests I'd like to explore?
- What qualities do I admire in my family, and which could be improved?
- How often do I communicate digitally vs. face-to-face, and does the medium matter to me?

REVIEW MOMENT

ARE THERE PROMPTS THAT HAVE BEEN PARTICULARLY CHALLENGING TO ANSWER? WHAT MAKES THEM DIFFICULT?

Not all reflection is easy. Identify any prompts that you've struggled with. Understanding why certain questions are difficult can help you target specific areas for growth or change.

Date ____________

- What are the strongest virtues I try to cultivate?
- How do my goals affect my daily routines and habits?
- Am I willing to unlearn beliefs or habits that are no longer useful?

Date ____________

- How would I describe my personal belief system?
- What steps have I taken to improve my mental health?
- Are there mentors or role models at work who inspire me?

Date ____________

- Are there spiritual or mindfulness practices I want to learn more about?
- What hobbies bring me the most joy and satisfaction?
- What is my relationship with substances like alcohol, tobacco, or caffeine?

Date ______

- How often do I feel like I have time just for myself?
- Are there workplace relationships that I should invest more in?
- Do I have a support system I can turn to when I'm feeling down?

Date ______

- What's a past contribution I'm particularly proud of?
- Do I have enough time for self-care and relaxation?
- How do our family dynamics impact my well-being?

Date ____________

- What are some of the things I've always wanted to do but haven't yet?
- How do I react when things don't go as planned?
- Do I have any adventure or exploration goals for this year?

Date ____________

- Do I feel like I'm in touch with my emotional self?
- How financially compatible am I with my partner or family?
- Do I prioritize my hobbies or do they get side-lined?

Date ____________

- Do I set clear boundaries between work time and personal time?
- What are some non-material things that make me happy?
- Am I too reliant on digital communication for socializing?

Date ____________

- What steps can I take to improve the quality of my social life?
- What social issues matter most to me?
- Am I keeping up with regular health check-ups and screenings?

Date ____________

- What role does exercise play in my life, and is it a positive one?
- How often do I engage in acts of kindness?
- What online or community resources do I use for learning?

Date ____________

- How do my relationships affect my mental and emotional state?
- How do new experiences make me feel?
- What are some character traits I'm proud of?

Date ____________

- Do I have any debts, and what's my plan for managing them?
- What are the consequences of not reaching my goals?
- How does my family handle crises or challenges?

Date ___________

- How does my inner life influence my daily actions?
- How often do I find myself in misunderstandings?
- What boundaries have I set, and are they respected?

Date ____________

- Am I willing to step out of my comfort zone to achieve my goals?
- How often do I find myself scrambling to meet deadlines?
- How have my values and priorities changed over time?

Date ____________

- What's one change I can make this week to improve my time management?
- Are there barriers that prevent me from being more active in community initiatives?
- How does my time management affect my stress levels?

Date ____________

- Do I share any hobbies with friends or family?
- What patterns of communication do I notice within my family?
- Are there any subscriptions or recurring expenses I can trim down?

Date ____________

- What are the consequences of not reaching my goals?
- Do I make learning a fun and engaging activity?
- How would I describe my personal belief system?

Date ____________

- What barriers keep me from being more creative?
- What are the common distractions that derail my focus and how can I manage them?
- Am I mindful of my emotional energy and where it goes?

Date ____________

- Do I engage in practices that promote mental clarity?
- Am I open to feedback, and do I use it as an opportunity for growth?
- Am I open to differing opinions and viewpoints?

Date ____________

- Are there differences in values or beliefs that cause tension?
- How do I prefer to learn: reading, watching, doing, or a mix?
- How often do I engage in acts of kindness?

Date ____________

- How often do I review and adjust my goals?
- Can I give more of my time, resources, or skills?
- Do I feel a sense of purpose or calling in life?

Date ____________

- Do I celebrate my achievements, no matter how small?
- Am I clear and concise when conveying my thoughts?
- What DIY project could I undertake to enhance my living space?

Date ____________

- How does my current role align with my long-term career goals?
- Do I feel like I have enough "me-time"?
- How do I handle setbacks or failures?

Date ______

- What patterns of communication do I notice within my family?
- How do I capture or record my adventures?
- What have I learned from my mistakes?

Date ______

- Do I prioritize my to-dos, or do I tend to react to what comes up?
- Is my current work-life balance sustainable?
- When was the last time I felt curious, and what triggered it?

Date

- Do I make time for self-reflection or mindfulness?
- Do my social activities align with my values and interests?
- Are there times when work seems to overshadow other areas of my life?

Date

- What self-care routines have I established, and how effective are they?
- What new social activities or groups would I like to explore?
- How do I keep up-to-date with news and trends in areas I care about?

REVIEW MOMENT

HAVE I NOTICED ANY PATTERNS OR THEMES IN MY RESPONSES ACROSS DIFFERENT AREAS?

Over time, you might notice recurring themes or patterns in your reflections. Acknowledging these patterns can help you understand your core values and areas that may need attention.

Date ____________

- Do I feel a sense of belonging in my social groups?
- Do I feel a need for more friendships or different types of relationships?
- Looking forward, what health and fitness goals would bring me a sense of contentment?

Date ____________

- How do I feel when I see positive changes happening in my community?
- Do I feel heard and understood by my family members?
- How do my hobbies align with my values and passions?

Date ____________

- Have I tried a new hobby or activity recently? What was it?
- What have I learned from my hobbies?
- Do I celebrate my achievements, no matter how small?

Date ____________

- Do I feel in control of my financial destiny?
- How has my style or approach to creativity evolved over time?
- Looking forward, what health and fitness goals would bring me a sense of contentment?

Date ____________

- How often do I set aside time for creative activities?
- Does my living space feel cluttered or disorganized?
- Do I make time for tasks that align with my long-term goals and values?

Date ____________

- What's one small step I can take this week to satisfy my curiosity in a particular area?
- Do I feel connected to my neighbourhood or local community?
- How do I deal with feelings of existential doubt or spiritual emptiness?

Date __________

- Do I have opportunities for promotion or lateral moves in my current role?
- What is my relationship with substances like alcohol, tobacco, or caffeine?
- Is there a balance between solitary and social hobbies?

Date __________

- Are there specific areas, like work or home, where I think my communication could improve?
- How do I handle conflicts within my friendships?
- How do I feel when I see positive changes happening in my community?

Date ____________

- What's a skill I've always wanted to learn?
- Do my relationships offer a good balance of give-and-take?
- How do I reinforce or apply new knowledge?

Date ____________

- What local organizations could benefit from my skills or time?
- How do I contribute to a positive family environment?
- Do I have plants or natural elements that contribute to a sense of well-being?

Date ____________

- Am I too reliant on digital communication for socializing?
- Am I good at estimating how long tasks will take?
- Do I support local businesses and initiatives?

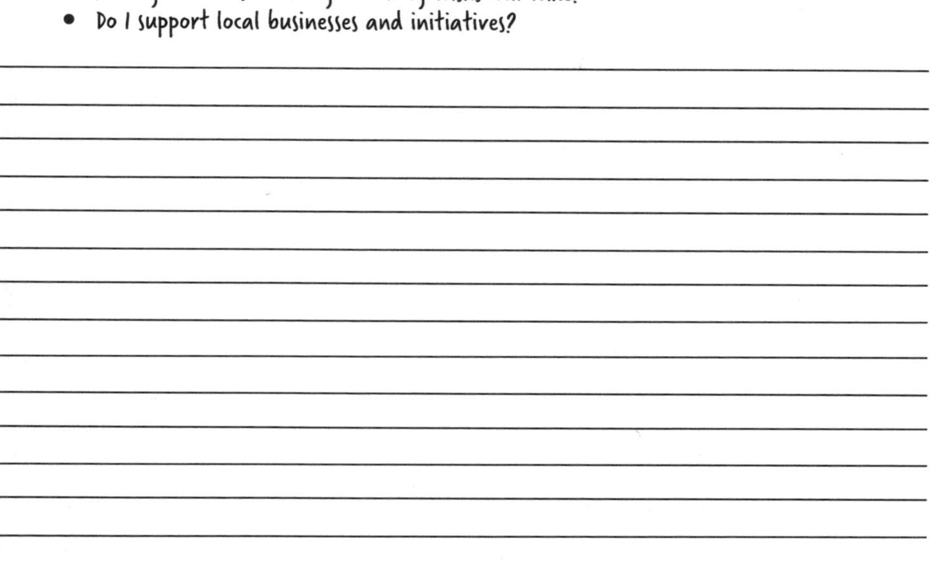

REVIEW MOMENT

WHAT AREA AM I MOST PROUD OF MY PROGRESS IN?

Celebrating your wins, no matter how small, is crucial for staying motivated. What achievements or progress are you particularly proud of? Revel in that positivity.

Date ____________

- Do I often initiate plans or wait to be invited?
- Do my hobbies allow me to express my creativity?
- Do I share my creative works with others? Why or why not?

Date ____________

- Am I open to differing opinions and viewpoints?
- Do I enjoy spontaneous trips or adventures?
- What practices help me find inner peace?

Date ______________

- Am I making the most of tax-advantaged savings accounts?
- How do I handle social pressures or expectations?
- Do I make time for self-directed learning outside of work or school?

Date ______________

- How have I grown professionally in the last year?
- Do my hobbies challenge me in beneficial ways?
- What is one emotional well-being goal I'd like to set for myself this month?

Date ___________

- How do I feel mentally and emotionally on most days?
- When was the last time I did something for the first time?
- What's one activity that I wish I had more time for?

Date ____________

- What resources could help me achieve my goals faster?
- Do I actively listen when someone else is speaking?
- How have I pushed myself out of my comfort zone lately?

Date ____________

- What hobbies bring me the most joy and satisfaction?
- What's one change I can make this week to improve my time management?
- What does "adventure" mean to me?

Date ______

- What acts of kindness have I engaged in recently?
- Do I set aside time for self-reflection and personal planning?
- How does my work-life balance affect my relationships?

Date ______

- How do I generally feel when I wake up in the morning?
- Am I afraid of judgment or criticism for my creative work?
- How do I feel when I check my bank account or financial statements?

Date ____________

- How do I handle conflicts within my friendships?
- Looking ahead, what changes or improvements would I like to see in my career?
- Do I feel heard and understood by my family members?

Date ___________

- How do I contribute to the well-being of my friends?
- Am I making enough time for exercise, sleep, and good nutrition?
- What's a subject or skill I've always wanted to explore?

Date ___________

- How do weekends and days off look for me? Restorative or just an extension of work?
- Do I feel supported and understood by the people around me?
- Do I feel connected to nature in my living environment?

Date ____________

- Do I feel a need for more friendships or different types of relationships?
- What are some ways I can be more eco-friendly?
- Do I have any unresolved conflicts at work, and what can I do about them?

Date ____________

- How well do I communicate under pressure?
- How accountable am I in pursuing my goals?
- Are there rituals or routines that enhance my sense of spiritual connection?

Date ___________

- Do I regularly celebrate my own progress, however small it may be?
- How does my current role align with my long-term career goals?
- How does the layout of my home affect its functionality?

REVIEW MOMENT

ARE THERE NEW HABITS OR ROUTINES THAT I'VE STARTED AS A RESULT OF MY REFLECTIONS?

Transformation often starts with small, everyday changes. Have you adopted any new habits or routines as a result of your time with the notebook? Recognize and celebrate these constructive shifts in your life.

Date ____________

- How do we handle conflict as a family?
- How fulfilled do I feel in my closest relationships?
- Are there any persistent health issues or symptoms that I should address?

Date ____________

- Are there people in my life who encourage my creativity?
- What self-care routines have I established, and how effective are they?
- Have I volunteered recently? How did it make me feel?

Date ____________

- Am I comfortable setting boundaries in different areas of my life?
- Am I proactive or reactive when it comes to health issues?
- How do we celebrate achievements or milestones?

Date ____________

- Do I regularly take the time to tidy or clean my living space?
- What cultural experiences have I always wanted to immerse myself in?
- Can I give more of my time, resources, or skills?

Date ___________

- Do I seek mentorship or guidance in achieving my objectives?
- Am I too reliant on digital communication for socializing?
- Are there people in my life who encourage my creativity?

Date ____________

- What would I like my lasting impact on society to be?
- What charitable giving or community support can I comfortably afford?
- What new skills have I learned recently?

Date ____________

- How do I capture or record my adventures?
- Do I make time for tasks that align with my long-term goals and values?
- How does my body language align with my verbal communication?

Date ____________

- How do I feel about my role in the family?
- What sounds fill my living space, and how do they affect me?
- Are there any new interests I'd like to explore?

Date ____________

- How do my hobbies align with my values and passions?
- How well do I maintain long-distance friendships?
- Are there barriers that prevent me from being more active in community initiatives?

Date ____________

- How do I contribute to the well-being of my friends?
- Do I tend to dominate conversations or hold back?
- What barriers keep me from being more creative?

Date ______

- What creative outlets bring me the most joy?
- Do I seek mentorship or guidance in achieving my objectives?
- How financially compatible am I with my partner or family?

Date ______

- Am I clear about why each goal is important to me?
- Are there any changes I'd like to make to my outdoor living space?
- Am I generally persuasive when I want to be?

Date ____________

- Do I have a "travel tribe" or people who encourage me to explore?
- Could I be a bridge in bringing different communities together?
- Do I tend to dominate conversations or hold back?

Date ____________

- How can I make my workspace more conducive to productivity, so work doesn't spill into personal time?
- What role does intimacy play in my life, and am I content with it?
- What does self-care look like for me?

Date ____________

- What future initiatives do I want to be a part of?
- Are there friendships that need rekindling?
- Do I have mentors or people I learn from regularly?

Date ______

- Do I have a support system that understands and respects my health goals?
- Do I have a go-to method for de-stressing after a long day?
- What social issues matter most to me?

Date ______

- What have I learned from my mistakes?
- How does my body language align with my verbal communication?
- Is my work-life balance conducive to my physical and mental well-being?

Date ____________

- Do I feel like I have enough "me-time"?
- Do I feel content with my current spiritual path?
- Is there a project or task that I'm particularly proud of recently?

Date ____________

- What small acts of kindness could I easily integrate into my daily life?
- Am I open to exploring different artistic mediums?
- How do the ethics and values of my workplace align with my own?

Date ____________

- How satisfied am I with my current social circle?
- Have I considered mentoring or teaching in my community?
- How do I handle setbacks or challenges in my health journey?

Date ____________

- How much time do I allocate for unplanned interruptions or delays?
- Are there opportunities for me to share my own culture or experiences with the community?
- Am I afraid of judgment or criticism for my creative work?

Date ____________

- Do I have a budget, and if so, how closely do I stick to it?
- Have I volunteered recently? How did it make me feel?
- Are there financial discussions or decisions I've been avoiding?

Date ______

- Are there hobbies I've neglected that I'd like to revisit?
- What would my ideal job look like?
- Are there any 'time sinks' in my personal life that could be better spent?

Date ______

- Am I proactive or reactive when it comes to health issues?
- Do I have a dedicated space for creative work?
- Am I able to say no to extra tasks or projects that would disrupt my work-life balance?

Date ___________

- What's a recent mistake, and what lesson did it teach me?
- How can I involve my family or friends in community activities?
- Do I enjoy spontaneous trips or adventures?

Date ____________

- Have I tried a new hobby or activity recently? What was it?
- Do I feel connected to something greater than myself?
- Do I have mentors, role models, or guides who enrich my perspective?

Date ____________

- Is there a diversity of perspectives and experiences within my social circle?
- How does my curiosity manifest in my daily life?
- Have I read a book or watched a film lately that transported me to another world?

REVIEW MOMENT

IS THERE SOMETHING I LEARNED ABOUT MYSELF THAT I WISH TO EXPLORE FURTHER?

Sometimes a single reflection can open a door to a new path or interest. Have you stumbled upon an area or topic that you're itching to delve deeper into?

Date ____________

- How often do I experience feelings of fatigue or burnout?
- What are some ways I can volunteer that align with my interests?
- Am I continually seeking to expand my horizons and learn new things?

Date ____________

- What could I do to strengthen that sense of community?
- How do I measure my own success, and is that metric fulfilling?
- How often do I engage in mindfulness practices like meditation or deep-breathing exercises?

Date ______

- Have I discovered any new forms of creativity recently?
- How does my inner life influence my daily actions?
- What are the consequences of not reaching my goals?

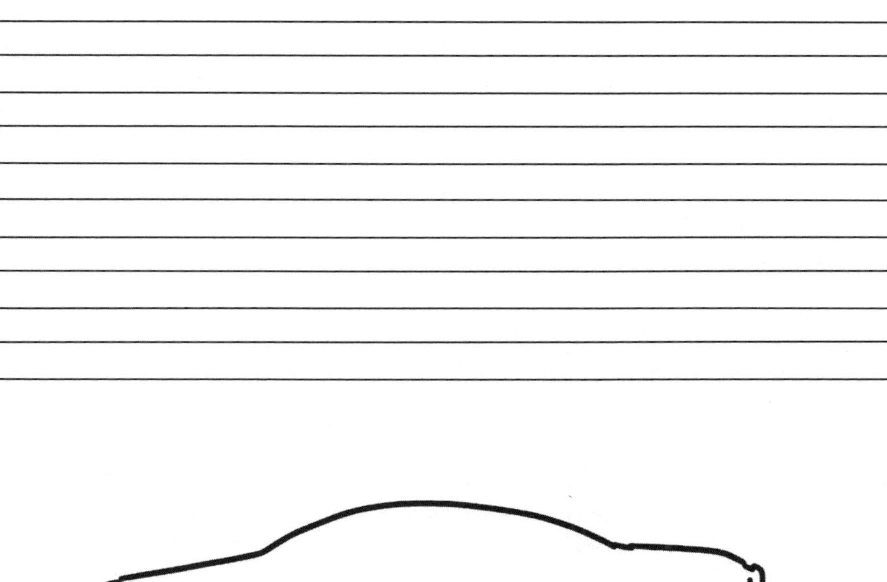

Date ____________

- Could I dedicate a specific amount of time each month to community involvement?
- Am I often late, and if so, why?
- What sounds fill my living space, and how do they affect me?

Date ____________

- Do the colours in my living space reflect the energy I want to cultivate?
- How can I involve my family or friends in community activities?
- How do I measure my own success, and is that metric fulfilling?

Date ______________

- Am I mindful of my emotional energy and where it goes?
- What's the one hobby I would pursue if time and money were not a constraint?
- How knowledgeable am I about financial topics, and where could I improve?

Date ______________

- What's a topic I'd like to know more about but have hesitated to dive into?
- What new skills have I learned recently?
- Have I tried a new hobby or activity recently? What was it?

Date ____________

- Do I feel connected to my neighbourhood or local community?
- Does my home feel like a sanctuary to me?
- Do my friends encourage my growth and well-being?

Date ____________

- How secure do I feel about my current financial situation?
- Looking forward, what health and fitness goals would bring me a sense of contentment?
- Are there any self-limiting beliefs holding me back?

Date ____________

- How have I pushed myself out of my comfort zone lately?
- Do I ever use my creativity to solve problems at work or home?
- Are there ways to include loved ones in my hobbies?

Date ____________

- How satisfied am I with my current level of physical fitness?
- Do I regularly take the time to tidy or clean my living space?
- How often do I review and adjust my goals?

Date ____________

- Am I satisfied with how much time I spend on leisure activities?
- How well do I manage my emotions while communicating?
- What could I do to strengthen that sense of community?

Date ____________

- How do I react to criticism or differing opinions?
- What's one activity that I wish I had more time for?
- How do my relationships affect my mental and emotional state?

Date ____________

- How well do I maintain long-distance friendships?
- How do our family dynamics impact my well-being?
- Do I use any tools or techniques to manage my time better?

Date ____________

- Do I have a go-to method for de-stressing after a long day?
- Could I dedicate a specific amount of time each month to community involvement?
- How effective am I at resolving conflicts through communication?

Date __________

- What's one small creative act I can do today?
- How do I react to criticism or differing opinions?
- How has my perspective broadened through past adventures?

Date __________

- Is there a difference between my public persona and my inner self?
- What's one step I could take right now toward a goal?
- How does my curiosity manifest in my daily life?

Date ____________

- Do I have a dedicated space for creative work?
- What is one emotional well-being goal I'd like to set for myself this month?
- How do I handle conflicts within my friendships?

Date ______________

- In what small ways do I contribute to my community?
- Do I prioritize my to-dos, or do I tend to react to what comes up?
- Do I feel content with my current spiritual path?

Date ______________

- How does my curiosity manifest in my daily life?
- Are there unresolved issues with family or friends that weigh on my mind?
- Am I satisfied with the quality of time spent with family?

Date ________

- Do I have any long-term learning goals?
- Are there any subscriptions or recurring expenses I can trim down?
- What's one new place I'd like to visit this year?

Date ________

- Are there ways to include loved ones in my hobbies?
- What steps can I take to nurture closer, healthier family relationships?
- Do my social activities align with my values and interests?

Date ______________

- What aspects of my job make me feel most fulfilled?
- How do I handle conflict within my relationships?
- Do I take time to understand others' viewpoints before responding?

Date ______________

- Are there any 'time sinks' in my personal life that could be better spent?
- How do we handle conflict as a family?
- Do I feel connected to something greater than myself?

Date ______________

- What traditions or rituals are important to our family identity?
- How often do I experience feelings of fatigue or burnout?
- How often do I step out of my comfort zone?

Date ___________

- Am I keeping up with regular health check-ups and screenings?
- How do I feel about my role in the family?
- Do my hobbies allow me to escape and recharge effectively?

Date ___________

- How do I contribute to the well-being of my friends?
- Do I tend to dominate conversations or hold back?
- What barriers keep me from being more creative?

REVIEW MOMENT

HAVE ANY OF THE PROMPTS LED TO MEANINGFUL ACTIONS OR CHANGES IN MY LIFE?

Reflection is most powerful when it leads to action. Have you made any significant changes in your life based on your answers to the prompts?

Date ____________

- How fulfilled do I feel in my closest relationships?
- What's stopping me from taking the next step towards a big adventure?
- Am I willing to step out of my comfort zone to achieve my goals?

Date __________

- Are there unresolved issues with family or friends that weigh on my mind?
- How do I feel when I first walk into my home?
- How satisfied am I with my current level of physical fitness?

Date __________

- Do the objects and decor in my home bring me joy?
- Are there tasks that consistently take longer than I expect?
- Am I comfortable with voicing my opinions and needs?

Date ____________

- Am I making enough time for exercise, sleep, and good nutrition?
- What boundaries have I set, and are they respected?
- How have I grown professionally in the last year?

Date ____________

- What small victories should I celebrate today?
- Do I have a sleep routine that leaves me feeling rested and rejuvenated?
- Do I set clear boundaries between work time and personal time?

Date ______

- What social issues matter most to me?
- What could I do to strengthen that sense of community?
- How do I feel about my role in the family?

Date ____________

- Do I feel heard and understood by my family members?
- Have I considered ethical aspects of my spending habits?
- Do the colours in my living space reflect the energy I want to cultivate?

Date ____________

- How do I deal with feelings of existential doubt or spiritual emptiness?
- Do my friends encourage my growth and well-being?
- What skills have I gained through my goal-achieving efforts?

Date ______________

- Have I considered mentoring or teaching in my community?
- Do I take time to understand others' viewpoints before responding?
- What's one small step I can take this week to satisfy my curiosity in a particular area?

Date ______________

- What activities help me unwind after a busy day at work?
- How does the lighting in my home affect my mood?
- Do I feel more energized or relaxed after expressing myself creatively?

- What's a subject or skill I've always wanted to explore?
- How have I grown professionally in the last year?
- Do I have a dedicated space for creative work?

Date ___________

Date ____________

- Do my friends encourage my growth and well-being?
- What emotions or thoughts frequently occupy my inner world?
- Do my work responsibilities play to my strengths?

Date ____________

- How often do I step out of my comfort zone?
- How often do I engage in mindfulness practices like meditation or deep-breathing exercises?
- Am I making enough time for exercise, sleep, and good nutrition?

Date ____________

- What aspects of communication do I find challenging?
- How often do I step out of my comfort zone to learn something new?
- How accountable am I in pursuing my goals?

Date ____________

- How do I handle creative blocks?
- How have I pushed myself out of my comfort zone lately?
- Am I happy with my eating habits, or are there changes I'd like to make?

Date ____________

- What DIY project could I undertake to enhance my living space?
- How comfortable do I feel in social settings?
- What's a small adventure I can go on this weekend?

Date ____________

- What steps can I take to achieve better work-life harmony?
- Do I have mentors or people I learn from regularly?
- Do I have a sleep routine that leaves me feeling rested and rejuvenated?

Date ____________

- What's the one hobby I would pursue if time and money were not a constraint?
- What physical activities bring me joy and fulfilment?
- How often do I set aside time for creative activities?

Date ____________

- What is one financial habit I'm proud of?
- What local organizations could benefit from my skills or time?
- Are there friendships or connections that I've neglected and wish to revive?

Date ____________

- What steps can I take if I feel like work is starting to encroach on my personal life?
- How does my creativity affect my emotional well-being?
- What patterns of communication do I notice within my family?

Date ____________

- How do I feel after spending time on my hobbies?
- Am I willing to unlearn beliefs or habits that are no longer useful?
- Are there aspects of my life where I feel stuck, and what can I do about it?

Date ______________

- How often do I step out of my comfort zone to learn something new?
- How have my values and priorities changed over time?
- How do I currently feel about my work-life balance?

Date ______________

- Who or what motivates me to reach my goals?
- How do I contribute to the well-being and happiness of others in my life?
- How am I investing in my own well-being and happiness?

Date ______________

- How does my living environment impact my daily routines?
- How do I feel after spending time on my hobbies?
- Am I open to exploring different artistic mediums?

Date ______________

- Do I feel connected to my body and listen to its needs?
- Do I give constructive feedback to others?
- Are there workplace relationships that I should invest more in?

Date ______________

- What steps can I take to better align my actions with my inner values?
- What DIY project could I undertake to enhance my living space?
- How often do I check my work emails or attend to work tasks outside of official work hours?

REVIEW MOMENT

WHAT AREA DO I FEEL NEEDS THE MOST ATTENTION RIGHT NOW?

Life is a juggling act, and sometimes we drop a ball. What aspect of your life do you feel is currently lacking and needs immediate attention?

Date ______________

- Do I feel content with my current spiritual path?
- When was the last time I felt curious, and what triggered it?
- Are there hobbies I've neglected that I'd like to revisit?

Date ______________

- What have I learned from my hobbies?
- Is there a project or task that I'm particularly proud of recently?
- Am I clear and concise when conveying my thoughts?

- When was the last time I felt curious, and what triggered it?
- Do I feel a sense of purpose or calling in life?
- What would my ideal job look like?

Date ______

- Are there mentors or role models at work who inspire me?
- How secure do I feel about my current financial situation?
- Looking ahead, what changes or improvements would I like to see in my career?

Date ____________

- What would my ideal job look like?
- How do my hobbies contribute to my overall well-being?
- How do we handle conflict as a family?

Date ______________

- Do I make learning a fun and engaging activity?
- What small acts of kindness could I easily integrate into my daily life?
- What steps have I taken to improve my mental health?

Date ______________

- Could I be a bridge in bringing different communities together?
- What traditions or rituals are important to our family identity?
- Are there causes or issues in my community that I'm passionate about?

Date ______________

- Do I feel connected to nature in my living environment?
- Could I benefit from setting more specific deadlines for my tasks?
- How does my creativity influence my perspective on the world?

Date ______________

- How do I show appreciation and love to those who matter most to me?
- Am I open to adapting or evolving my hobbies over time?
- How does giving back to the community make me feel?

Date ___________

- Are there workplace relationships that I should invest more in?
- Do I feel a sense of community and belonging in my social circles?
- How often do I check in with myself emotionally?

Date ____________

- Do I ask for feedback on how I can communicate better?
- What financial milestones have I reached, and what's next on the horizon?
- Do I feel connected to something greater than myself?

Date ____________

- Does my living space feel cluttered or disorganized?
- Do I have any adventure or exploration goals for this year?
- Are there toxic or draining relationships that I should reconsider?

Date ________

- Are there tasks that consistently take longer than I expect?
- What changes do I wish to see in society?
- How often do I practice gratitude?

Date ________

- Is it easy for me to "switch off" from work mode when I'm at home?
- Am I open to the idea of solo adventures?
- How does the lighting in my home affect my mood?

Date ____________

- How do my hobbies contribute to my overall well-being?
- Do I feel a sense of duty or obligation, and is it balanced?
- How fulfilled do I feel in my closest relationships?

Date ____________

- What can I do to make my home more peaceful?
- Am I comfortable with voicing my opinions and needs?
- How informed am I about current events and social issues?

Date ____________

- What cultural experiences have I always wanted to immerse myself in?
- How do I feel when I see positive changes happening in my community?
- Do I share what I learn with others?

Date ____________

- How do my spending habits align with my values?
- Am I happy with my eating habits, or are there changes I'd like to make?
- Does my home feel like a sanctuary to me?

Date ____________

- Do I prioritize my hobbies or do they get side-lined?
- What does "adventure" mean to me?
- How often do I find myself scrambling to meet deadlines?

Date ______________

- Do I feel more energized or relaxed after expressing myself creatively?
- What goals have I set for myself this year?
- Do I feel a need for more friendships or different types of relationships?

Date ____________

- What are some ways I can be more eco-friendly?
- Have I considered turning a hobby into a side hustle?
- What aspects of communication do I find challenging?

Date ____________

- How often do I engage in deep, meaningful conversations?
- How often do I review and adjust my goals?
- Do I feel supported and uplifted by my friends?

Date ______

- Are there rituals or routines that enhance my sense of spiritual connection?
- What is one financial habit I'm proud of?
- How do I feel about my current communication skills?

Date ______

- What's one action I can take this week to improve my communication skills?
- Have I read a book or watched a film lately that transported me to another world?
- Are there tasks that I could delegate or outsource to free up more time?

Date ____________

- Are my investments diversified to help me meet my future needs?
- Do I prioritize my hobbies or do they get side-lined?
- What future initiatives do I want to be a part of?

Date ________

- Am I investing time in deepening existing relationships?
- Am I saving adequately for short-term and long-term goals?
- Am I often late, and if so, why?

Date ________

- What charitable giving or community support can I comfortably afford?
- What's a past contribution I'm particularly proud of?
- How well do I maintain long-distance friendships?

REVIEW MOMENT

HAVE MY GOALS OR PRIORITIES CHANGED SINCE I STARTED USING THIS NOTEBOOK?

our lives are in constant flux, and our priorities can change accordingly. Consider if your original goals or priorities have evolved since you began this journey.

Date ____________

- Am I investing time in deepening existing relationships?
- Am I saving adequately for short-term and long-term goals?
- Am I often late, and if so, why?

Date ____________

- What charitable giving or community support can I comfortably afford?
- What's a past contribution I'm particularly proud of?
- How well do I maintain long-distance friendships?

Date ____________

- What charitable giving or community support can I comfortably afford?
- How often do I feel like I have time just for myself?
- How has my style or approach to creativity evolved over time?

Date ____________

- How does the lighting in my home affect my mood?
- How often do I reassess my daily or weekly schedule?
- What goals have I set for myself this year?

Date ____________

- What organizations or causes would I like to support?
- Are there unresolved issues that need addressing?
- Are there spiritual or mindfulness practices I want to learn more about?

Date ____________

- What's a creative project I've been putting off?
- How do I maintain a balance between my inner and outer worlds?
- How do I prefer to learn: reading, watching, doing, or a mix?

Date ____________

- How do I balance ambition with contentment?
- How often do I engage in deep, meaningful conversations?
- What personal goals have I set for myself, and what's my plan to achieve them?

Date ____________

- Do I share my creative works with others? Why or why not?
- How does my current lifestyle fit within my income?
- Am I excited to go to work most days, or is it a struggle?

Date ____________

- Looking ahead, what relationship goals would help me feel more content?
- Are there tasks that I could delegate or outsource to free up more time?
- How does my current role align with my long-term career goals?

Date ____________

- Are there any financial worries that keep me up at night?
- How much of my identity is tied to my career, and is that okay with me?
- Do I feel supported and understood by the people around me?

Date ____________

- Am I happy with my eating habits, or are there changes I'd like to make?
- Are there ways to include loved ones in my hobbies?
- Do I make time for self-reflection or mindfulness?

Date ____________

- Am I prepared for a financial emergency or unexpected expenses?
- What sounds fill my living space, and how do they affect me?
- What's one change I can make this week to improve my time management?

Date ____________

- How often do I dedicate time to my hobbies?
- Am I comfortable setting boundaries in different areas of my life?
- How do I feel when I first walk into my home?

Date ______

- How do I handle moral or ethical dilemmas?
- What's a subject or skill I've always wanted to explore?
- Am I proactive or reactive when it comes to health issues?

Date ______

- What are some character traits I'm proud of?
- How does my time management impact people around me?
- Do the objects and decor in my home bring me joy?

Date ______________

- What does self-care look like for me?
- What creative achievements am I most proud of?
- Are there differences in values or beliefs that cause tension?

Date ______________

- How accountable am I in pursuing my goals?
- How do I currently feel about my work-life balance?
- Am I saving adequately for short-term and long-term goals?

Date ___________

- What skills would I like to develop to advance in my career?
- What small victories should I celebrate today?
- How do I maintain boundaries in my relationships?

Date ______________

- How do new experiences make me feel?
- How has my involvement in the community enriched my life?
- Do I engage in practices that promote mental clarity?

Date ______________

- Am I open to feedback, and do I use it as an opportunity for growth?
- Am I fairly compensated for the work I do?
- Do I support local businesses and artists in my community?

Date ________

- What are some happy memories that bring the family together?
- How has my perspective broadened through past adventures?
- Do I make learning a fun and engaging activity?

Date ________

- Am I good at estimating how long tasks will take?
- Are my investments diversified to help me meet my future needs?
- What new social activities or groups would I like to explore?

Date ____________

- Looking ahead, what changes or improvements would I like to see in my career?
- Are there any self-limiting beliefs holding me back?
- Have I considered ethical aspects of my spending habits?

Date ________

- Do I feel a sense of duty or obligation, and is it balanced?
- How often do I communicate digitally vs. face-to-face, and does the medium matter to me?
- What's stopping me from taking the next step towards a big adventure?

Date ________

- Have I volunteered recently? How did it make me feel?
- How do I keep up-to-date with news and trends in areas I care about?
- How does my creativity affect my emotional well-being?

Date ____________

- How do I contribute to the well-being and happiness of others in my life?
- Do I have any long-term learning goals?
- Is there a local issue that I feel strongly about and want to address?

Date ____________

- How do I maintain a positive mindset when faced with challenges?
- What practices help me find inner peace?
- What are some ways I can volunteer that align with my interests?

REVIEW MOMENT

HOW HAS USING THE CONTENTMENT NOTEBOOK IMPACTED MY DAILY MOOD OR GENERAL OUTLOOK?

The ultimate goal is a sense of well-being. Has consistent reflection and self-evaluation led to a noticeable change in your daily mood or your perspective on life?

Date ____________

- How has my style or approach to creativity evolved over time?
- Do I have a support system I can turn to when I'm feeling down?
- Do my relationships offer a good balance of give-and-take?

Date ____________

- What practices help me find inner peace?
- Do I feel guilty taking time off work? If so, why?
- Have I received constructive feedback lately, and how have I acted on it?

Date ____________

- Are there aspects of my life where I feel stuck, and what can I do about it?
- What's a recent mistake, and what lesson did it teach me?
- How financially compatible am I with my partner or family?

Date ____________

- Are there friendships that need rekindling?
- Are there any small changes I can make to improve my living environment?
- Could I benefit from setting more specific deadlines for my tasks?

Date ____________

- How can I make my living space more eco-friendly?
- How do I feel about my current communication skills?
- What are the milestones or achievements I'm most proud of this year?

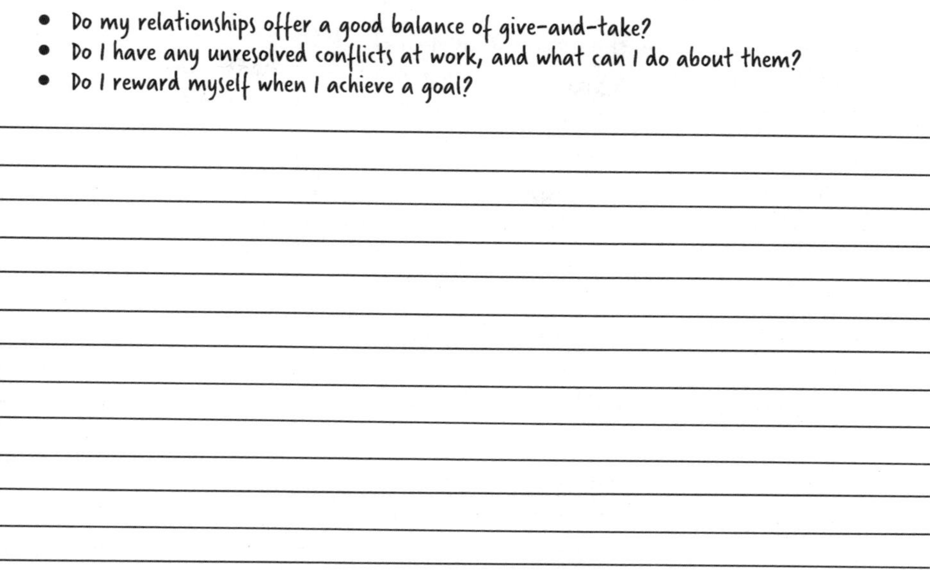

Date ____________

- Do my relationships offer a good balance of give-and-take?
- Do I have any unresolved conflicts at work, and what can I do about them?
- Do I reward myself when I achieve a goal?

Date ____________

- How do I react when things don't go as planned?
- Am I open to differing opinions and viewpoints?
- Is there a local issue that I feel strongly about and want to address?

Date ____________

- Do I use any tools or techniques to manage my time better?
- What are some happy memories that bring the family together?
- What self-care routines have I established, and how effective are they?

Date ______________

- Am I open to the idea of solo adventures?
- How do I educate myself on issues of social justice?
- How often do I reassess my daily or weekly schedule?

Date ______________

- What skills have I gained through my goal-achieving efforts?
- Do my work responsibilities play to my strengths?
- Am I open to the idea of solo adventures?

Date ____________

- How often do I engage in acts of kindness?
- How do I handle creative blocks?
- How do my spending habits align with my values?

REVIEW MOMENT

WHAT AM I MOST GRATEFUL FOR IN THIS JOURNEY TOWARD CONTENTMENT?

Gratitude can be a powerful catalyst for happiness. As you reflect, what are you most thankful for in this personal journey you've embarked on?

REFLECTING ON YOUR JOURNEY: A CLOSING NOTE

As you reach the final pages of "The Contentment Notebook," take a moment to appreciate the journey you've embarked upon. Over the days, weeks, or even months, you've delved deep into various aspects of your life, uncovering insights and discovering new facets of yourself. We hope this notebook has been more than just a collection of prompts; it's been a companion on your path to understanding contentment.

Celebrating Your Progress

Reflect on the progress you've made. You've explored areas like career satisfaction, financial health, personal relationships, and more, each offering its unique lens to view your life. Think about the moments of realization, the shifts in perspective, and the small victories you've celebrated along the way. Each entry in this notebook has been a step towards a more fulfilled and balanced life.

Carrying Contentment Forward

The habit of reflection you've cultivated is a precious tool that will continue to serve you. Remember, contentment isn't a destination but a continuous journey. As you move forward, carry the insights and lessons learned with you. They will be your guide in times of uncertainty and a source of joy in moments of celebration.

Your Notebook, Your Story

Your entries in this notebook are the narrative of your journey toward contentment. They are uniquely yours, filled with hopes, challenges, successes, and dreams. As you close this notebook, know that your story of contentment doesn't end here. It's a lifelong journey, and you have the power to shape it each day.

A Last Word of Encouragement

Keep this notebook as a reminder of your journey and the progress you've made. Revisit it when you need a boost of motivation or a moment of reflection. Most importantly, remember that the pursuit of contentment is an ongoing, ever-evolving process. You are equipped with the insights and wisdom to continue making choices that enrich your life and the lives of those around you.

Made in the USA
Middletown, DE
01 December 2024